THE TIME VALUE
OF LIFE

THE TIME VALUE OF LIFE:

WHY TIME IS MORE VALUABLE THAN MONEY

TISA L. SILVER, MBA

iUniverse, Inc.
New York   Bloomington

iUniverse books may be ordered through booksellers or by contacting:

iUniverse
1663 Liberty Drive
Bloomington, IN 47403
www.iuniverse.com
1-800-Authors (1-800-288-4677)

Because of the dynamic nature of the Internet, any Web addresses or links
contained in this book may have changed since publication and may no longer be
valid. The views expressed in this work are solely those of the author and do not
necessarily reflect the views of the publisher, and the publisher hereby disclaims
any responsibility for them.

ISBN: 978-1-4401-3480-7 (sc)
ISBN: 978-1-4401-3481-4 (ebook)
ISBN: 978-1-4401-3482-1 (dj)

Library of Congress Control Number: 2009926408

Printed in the United States of America

iUniverse rev. date: 7/7/2009

To all who invested in me. I hope to pay it forward.

Contents

ACKNOWLEDGMENTS

I would like to thank my parents, Ezel and Sherrilyn, and my sister, Kia, for their support. This book contains some of the most difficult lessons of my life. Thank you for helping me get through them.

I would also like to thank my grandparents, Lucille Silver and Wayne and Marjorie Smith, for showing me the value of hard work and independence.

I would like to express my gratitude to Crystal Simms for lending her ear and expertise. Thank you for pushing me to share my story.

Finally, I would like to thank God for blessing me so richly.

All graphics have been illustrated by author.

INTRODUCTION

In many other self-help books, people tell you about life-changing events and how they have motivated them to vow never to smoke again, or cheat again—whatever it may be. Their lives were made complete because of this one thing that they discovered and now want to share with you. This is not that type of book. I have no cookie-cutter solutions to solving your problems, because no such solutions exist.

I wrote this book to share how a simple decision-making rule used in finance can be applied to making decisions in other areas of life, especially decisions about how you will use the time you have been given on this earth. If you can persevere through some introductory level finance lessons, you can easily learn a few life lessons about time. My hope is that you will learn from my experiences (and mistakes), and treat time like the valuable gift that it is.

The lessons I offer come from my background as a student-turned-professor-of-finance, and from my own experience with life. There are many parallels between finance and life, and between money and time.

A series of events in my past, including the dream introduced in the prologue—whose ending I will visit later—has caused me to view the values of time and money differently.

There is no way to put a value on life, because our existence is impossible to quantify. Quite often, however, we try to measure that value using the gauge of time. We treasure our lives in minutes, hours, days, months, and years.

Every day, we also see instances where a monetary value is placed on time. So, we will start with a basic model called the Time Value of Money (TVM). The TVM model has four components: the present value (PV), return (r), time (t), and the future value (FV).

This book contains several "what-if" examples using TVM calculations. Some examples include investments in stocks and bonds, while others explore the value of lottery jackpots and opening a business. I will provide the answers, though I still recommend that you work through them with a financial calculator. You can use these examples as practice and apply the methods to solve your own financial "what-if" scenarios.

Speaking of calculators, when I was a child, my dad would often pull a burgundy-and-tan book out of a kitchen cabinet. It was full of numbers, and I always wondered what he was looking at. I later learned that it was an amortization schedule, which serves the same purpose as a calculator but takes much more time!

If you have ever taken out a loan, bought a car or house, or purchased anything on credit (or even if you plan to do so in the future), you *need* to own a financial calculator, so that you can know what to expect before you close any major deals by making important calculations.

PROLOGUE: THE DREAM

It was a Wednesday evening in the spring of 2006. I had just finished teaching a long day of classes, and I had stopped by to visit my former boyfriend's family. On this particular evening, he was also there. It was rare that Michael and I happened to be at his aunt's house at the same time. Even though we weren't together anymore, we had remained friends.

I made my living room rounds, giving hugs and kisses to all of his aunts. Then, from his great aunt's chair, Michael turned to me with his arms outstretched and lips puckered. I was seeing someone else at the time, so I let my head (which told me to be respectful) overrule my heart (which told me to go for it). I playfully smacked him on the arm and said, "You know better!" Everybody laughed and we went on to have a pleasant visit.

When we walked out to the front yard, we made small talk and then he said, "I have a proposition for you." I asked what it was, and he explained that his little sister's birthday was a little over a month away and he wanted to surprise her. He asked if I would come with them to Busch Gardens or Kings Dominion to celebrate her birthday if he paid for two hotel rooms. This time my head said, "No," but my heart said, "Yes"—and so did my mouth!

For a long time I had known that I was going to cut things off with my other friend, John. However, John had a lot of things going wrong in his life, and I didn't want to kick him while he was down. The month between now and the birthday trip would be enough time for me to end that relationship. Then I'd be free to enjoy this surprise trip with no guilt. After I accepted, Michael told me that he would give me a call and we would work out the dates.

During the week after the invitation, I had problems sleeping every night. My heart would beat so fast that I thought my chest would burst. Occasionally, it was as though something was cutting off my air. I couldn't breathe. This kind of thing had happened to me before, but usually right before boarding a plane. The last time I had that feeling was the previous summer, when I'd had another dream about him. That dream had ended with me inside his aunt's house, while outside, two police officers—one male and one female—knocked on the door.

CHAPTER ONE: TIME AND MONEY

I hate to begin a chapter with lots of questions, but I want you to think about how you treat your time and your money. Give some thought to the following questions:

Would you lend money to someone?

Would it matter who that "someone" was?

Would you expect to be repaid more than the amount you loaned (interest)?

Would it matter how long that "someone" took to repay the loan?

Your answers to these questions will tell you four things about yourself: whether you are willing to sacrifice, for whom you are willing to sacrifice, how long you are willing to sacrifice, and how much you expect in return for your sacrifice.

Now, answer the questions again, replacing the word "money" with the word "time." Did your answers change?

You probably had trouble, because the questions have to change in order to suit time. So, here is a new set of questions that may be more appropriate:

Would you give someone your time?

Would it matter who that "someone" was?

Would you expect anything in return?

> *Would it matter how long that "someone" took to repay*
> *you for your time?*

Take a look at your answers. Which set has more stipulations?

Unlike money, you cannot lend time, and whoever receives your time will never be able to give it back. Money is a renewable, replaceable commodity, but time is not. So why do we treat our money with such care and our time with such indifference?

The most commonly used phrase containing time and money is a simple one—*time is money*. This implies equality between the two entities, but the relationship between time and money can be much more complicated. Consider the following truth.

You Must Spend Time in Order to Make Money

Think about your job. Although the amount of money you make depends on your pay structure, generally speaking, the more time you spend working, the more money you make. For wage or contract workers, putting in more time results in a direct increase in pay and perhaps overtime. For salaried workers, more time spent working will perhaps lead to a bonus. For those in sales, the more time you spend attracting new customers and maintaining relationships with existing ones, the more money you make.

I would like to revisit the wage worker scenario and encourage you to think about the concept of overtime. Let's suppose that your normal schedule allows for a forty-hour workweek. This week, you choose to work one additional hour. If your company pays overtime, you will be paid time-and-a-half, which is 150 percent of your normal hourly rate. By paying you time-and-a-half, your company is sending you a clear message: the forty-first hour is worth more than each of the previous forty. Why? Because your employer understands that time has value, and that extra time has extra value.

Can You Spend Money to Make Time?

Unfortunately, the relationship between time and money does not go both ways. You can spend time to make money, but you can't spend money to make more time. However, *making more money can provide more choices for how you spend time.*

A lot of people think that life would be easier if only they had more money, but I disagree. More money often leads to more problems.

When you make more money, you pay more taxes, and, depending on how you made the money, your taxes may be more complicated to determine. The added wealth increases the likelihood that you will need the services of a professional to greet Uncle Sam when he comes for his share.

Time is more valuable than money. Both can be spent, but only one can be replaced.

When people think you have nothing, they tend not to ask you for much. When you make more money, sometimes old friends and long-lost relatives emerge suddenly, wanting to take an interest in your life. I have seen it happen with professional athletes frequently. A while ago, I watched a TV special on lottery winners that was quite sad. For many of the winners, the very prize they thought would save them turned out to be their downfall. Some couldn't cope with the attention, while others became paranoid because they didn't know if they could ever trust anyone. Some turned to crime and other destructive behavior. Many of them wasted their entire fortunes.

Even though I started out with some negatives, we all know that there is definitely a positive side to having more money. Having more money can provide you with more flexibility. If

3

you want to take a vacation, instead of going to Florida you can go to France. In France, having more money would allow you to stay at the Ritz instead of at the Holiday Inn. In terms of time, more money could allow you to take one or two weeks instead of four days.

Does Making More Time Give You More Choices for How to Spend Your Money?

Once again, we have a relationship that cannot be reciprocated. The problem here is obvious: you can't make more time. All you can do is choose which parts of your life to devote more time to, or less time, but you can never create more time.

Does More Time Equal More Problems?

I have never heard anyone say, "The more time I have, the more problems I see," or, "Love of time is the root of all evil." It just doesn't make sense. If anything, people are constantly complaining about the need for more time to get rid of problems!

I can't count how many times I have heard the phrase, "Time is money." I understand what people mean when they say it, but the statement does not begin to address all of the intricacies in the relationship between time and money. It implies that time and money hold the same value. Time can be used to make money and making more money can provide flexibility with time, but you can't make more time.

It is for this reason that time is more valuable than money. Both can be spent, but only one can be replaced.

CHAPTER TWO: THE TIME VALUE OF MONEY

Which would you take: a dollar today or the promise of a dollar tomorrow?

You should take the dollar today. Aside from the fact that promises are often broken, an old English proverb says, "A bird in hand is better than two in the bush."

This is the basis for the Time Value of Money. If you wait for that dollar tomorrow, you may not get it. If you do get it, you should get more than the dollar to compensate for the delay.

Suppose you only have $100 and you lend it to a friend who promises to repay you in one week. During that week, you see a shirt you want to buy for $20, but you can't purchase *Your sacrifice is worth something, and that something is called interest.* the shirt because your friend has borrowed your money. You then see a pair of shoes for $30, and there is only one pair left in your size. You can't buy the shoes, though, because someone has borrowed your money.

Next you find out that your favorite artist is coming to town and tickets go on sale this week. The ticket costs $50, but you can't buy the ticket because you don't have the money. Or, if you are not a shopper, let's suppose someone offers you an investment that will take your one hundred dollars and give you one hundred and five dollars one week later. You can't reap the five-dollar profit, though, because you don't have the money to invest.

Whether it was shopping or investing, in each situation you had the opportunity but not the means to buy or invest in something that you wanted. You didn't have the money because you loaned it to a friend.

When the loan is repaid, you still may not be able to buy the shirt, shoes or concert tickets. Perhaps you will, but there is also the possibility that they will be all sold out. Also, the investment may no longer be available, or is now offering only four dollars instead of five. You delayed or denied yourself satisfaction so that your friend could be satisfied. Your sacrifice is worth something, and that something is called interest.

Saving money in a bank is a form of sacrifice. When you save money at a bank, the bank uses your deposits to make loans to other individuals and businesses. The bank receives interest on those loans. The loans would not be possible without your savings. By saving money, you are sacrificing purchases and potential investments. Your sacrifice allows the bank to make investments, which will make them more than enough money to pay you back. Banks can't make money without using your money, so they pay you to save.

Here is the TVM equation and an explanation of its inputs:

$$FV = PV(1 + r)^t$$
PV = present value
FV = future value
t = time
r = rate of return (%)

The loose interpretation of the formula is as follows: Invest PV and you will earn r for each period. At the end of t periods, you will have FV.

I use timelines like the following one whenever I have to solve TVM problems.

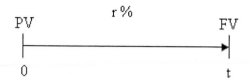

If you know any three of the TVM variables, you can solve for the fourth. Let's take a look at a few examples.

Finding Your Future Value, FV

Finding your future value is useful when you know how much you have to invest and you want to determine what you can end up with.

Suppose you placed one thousand dollars in a savings account this morning. The account will pay a 5 percent rate of return each year. You plan to invest the money for one year. How much money will you have at the end of that year?

$$FV = PV \times (1 + r)^t$$
$$FV = 1000 \times (1 + .05)^1 = 1000 \times 1.05 = \$1,050.00$$

At the end of one year you will have $1,050. You invested $1,000 in principal and you earned $50 in interest.

Finding Your Present Value, PV

Finding your present value is useful when you have a goal in mind for the future and you need to determine what to invest today to meet that goal.

Suppose you want to have $1,250 three years from now. You can invest the money in an account that will pay a 6.5 percent rate of return each year. How much money do you need to invest today to meet your goal?

$$FV = PV \times (1 + r)^t$$

$1,250 = PV \times (1.065)^3$
$1,250 = 1.20795 \times PV$
$PV = \$1,250/1.20795 = \$1,034.81$

You need to invest $1,034.81 in principal today in order to have $1,250 at the end of three years.

The present value and the future value are pretty easy to solve for, but the math gets trickier when you have to solve for the rate of return or the number of periods.

You will need to compute these numbers at some point in your life, and you can either buy a financial calculator or a book that has amortization schedules.

Finding the Rate of Return

r = return

Finding the rate of return is useful when you want to determine the percentage your investment must earn each period in order to meet your goal.

Let's suppose you are planning to send your youngest child to college. Your child is three years old and will start college at the age of eighteen. You have ten thousand dollars today and you want to have seventy thousand dollars in fifteen years.

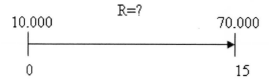

$$FV = PV (1 + r)^t$$

When solving for "r," doing the math by hand is difficult. By using my financial calculator, I can tell you that you would need an investment that paid a steady annual return of 13.85 percent.

Finding the Number of Periods

t = the number of time periods

Finding the number of periods lets you know how many years (or other time periods) over which you will need to invest.

Let's suppose that you want to be a millionaire. You have fifty thousand dollars today and an investment that offers a 12 percent annual rate of return. How long will it take for you to reach your goal?

$$FV = PV (1 + r)^t$$
$$1,000,000 = 50,000 \times (1 + .12)^t$$

You will have to take my word for it that solving for "t" will require a calculator! Solving the equation, we find that it would take you 26.43 years to reach your goal.

Now that we have identified the variables, let's explore them on a deeper level.

CHAPTER THREE: THE FUTURE VALUE

FV = future value

The future value is the amount of money you will have at some point in the future after making your initial investment. The future value is often called the *terminal value*, as it is the ending value of your investment. The future value is denominated in the same unit as the present value.

The future value does not have to be in dollars; it can be in any unit you choose to make it.

Let's suppose you are a seamstress capable of producing eight hundred dresses each year. Demand for your dresses begins to grow and you need to keep up. You have done your research and you expect demand to grow at 10 percent per year. How many dresses will you have to produce in five years?

$$FV = PV (1 + r)^t$$

$$FV = 800 (1.10)^5$$
$$FV = 1,288.41 \text{ or } 1,289 \text{ dresses}$$

By solving for the future value, you can now decide what you need to do to keep up with demand. In this case, you may have to purchase new machinery or hire additional workers. Planning ahead can prepare your business for the future.

Living from Day to Day

I was watching the news on Thanksgiving Day in 2005. A sports reporter asked a Washington Redskins running back, Clinton Portis, what he was thankful for. Portis said that he was thankful for his life because he never imagined himself living longer than twenty or twenty-five years. In the past I've been skeptical when I've heard that remark, but I really believed Portis. His statements became even more real to me after the tragic death of his young and talented teammate, Sean Taylor, who was murdered in a botched home invasion. The thought of someone really feeling that pessimistic about his life expectancy hurt my heart. Sadly, many people share Portis' sense of doom. They don't realize that they have the power to make initial investments of time and effort in their lives today that will result in greater rewards in their lives tomorrow.

Since my childhood, plans have been made *for* me, and eventually *by* me, for my future. My parents set up a savings account and purchased bonds for me to use when I went to college. I took the SAT in the seventh grade just to get practice for the real thing in high school. I am so thankful for the long-term thinkers God placed in my life!

Many kids are not so blessed, and as a result, they are concerned only about how they will spend the next few days. They bring true meaning to the phrase, "One day at a time." Each decision regarding their time, their money, and their actions is based on all things immediate. I hope you do not feel this way, but if you do, let me ask you this: what happens when you reach sixty-five and you have been living each day just for the moment?

At sixty-five, those who have planned ahead will be retiring, whereas you will have to continue to work or rely on your children to take care of you. Lack of long-term planning can result in your long- and short-term lifestyles being identical—working to meet obligations. The only thing that will certainly be different (and probably not in a positive way), is your health. Planning ahead helps both you and your loved ones.

A dear friend of mine passed away in a terrible accident at a young age. He had started a new job less than a year before his death. With every new job, a stack of papers awaits. You have to select options for health plans, retirement contributions, and insurance forms. On the life insurance policy offered by his job, he left the beneficiary line blank.

You can save your loved ones time and money by paying close attention to these forms and making sure they are completed.

When making his funeral arrangements, his family assumed that his insurance would cover it. My friend had adequate life insurance to cover the costs, but since there was no beneficiary listed, no one could access the money in time for his service. Months and mounds of paperwork later, the money was placed into an account for the benefit of his next of kin.

You can also help your loved ones by writing a will. When someone dies with no will, it places friends and families in awkward positions. Think of all of the things you have accumulated over the course of your life. Now think about how you would distribute the important things and dispose of everything else. If you do not leave any instructions behind, you force your loved ones to make these decisions for you. I can tell you from personal experience that it is a very stressful and painful process.

When my friend passed away, I thought it was so strange that what had taken him a lifetime to accumulate would be divided up or disposed of in a matter of days. It was hard to decide what to give away and what to keep. It was impossible to keep everything, but how do you decide what is worth saving and what isn't? While throwing away his things, I felt like we were, piece by piece, erasing every physical indication of his existence.

Taking a few minutes today can save your loved ones a lot of time, additional stress, and pain later.

"Then What? Moments"

Taking some time to think about what we are doing

financially and why we are doing it can benefit us in many ways.

In 1899, Thorstein Veblen published *The Theory of the Leisure Class*[1]. In this book (his most popular), he wrote about conspicuous consumption. Webster defines this term as "buying expensive services and products in order to flaunt your wealth." Think about the conspicuous purchases you may have made, and think about why you made them.

I have never been one for fancy things. In fact, some of my favorite indulgences include costume jewelry from Kohl's and one tote bag from the Coach outlet in Rehoboth Beach, Delaware!

Even though I haven't acted upon the fleeting urges I have sometimes had (like wanting to buy a Mercedes right out of graduate school), I can see why many people do so. Fancy clothes and cars attract attention, and the appearance of wealth impresses other people.

When I was in high school, the Polo brand was "in." I had one or two pieces of Polo from an outlet, but my grandmother made my day when she bought me a heavy zip-up sweatshirt with "USA" across the front and "Polo" on the sleeve. When she gave it to me, I wore it a few times thinking that everybody would see that "this is Polo." It has been twelve years since she gave me that sweatshirt and today I wear it because it keeps me warm.

I remember kids I went to school with who always wore the latest trends. I opted for basic clothes that would last longer than the trends. Back then it was probably because I was cheap, not necessarily enlightened! I took any little bit of money I got and saved it. Anyway, kids can't be held fully accountable for things like this since their money often comes from their parents, but now I see adults who act the same way. Everything has to have either some brand name plastered all over it or an easily visible or recognizable logo.

Why do we do this? As Veblen said over a hundred years

ago, people buy things to impress other people.[1] Maybe people do it to prove to others that they can afford the finer things, or because they think that showing off the finer things will cause others to treat them differently. Before you make a purchase motivated by what you assume others' reactions will be, ask yourself a simple question: "Then what?"

For example, "I will spend $700 on this handbag. It is so nice that people will stare at me. And then what?"

Here's what. They will go on with their lives and it will probably take them a few minutes or maybe a few hours to forget you and the bag. If they went home and fantasized about the handbag and told all of their friends about it, would this benefit you? Would it add value to your life? The fanfare has nothing to do with you. Even if it did have something to do with you, what difference would it make? The fleeting attention of strangers adds no value to your life. In fact, it costs you both today and in the future. Impress yourself. You will be wealthier for it.

Delayed gratification is worth the sacrifice of investing today.

I am not judging peoples' decisions, tastes, or the products they buy, but these purchases do nothing other than transfer wealth from those who need it to those who couldn't care less where it comes from.

This type of appearance-driven existence will take money from you instead of making money for you. Have you ever heard of a person buying a car for fifty thousand dollars, using the car for a few years, and then selling it for sixty thousand dollars—or for any price above fifty thousand dollars? Have you ever seen an old, used, designer suitcase on eBay selling for more than its original purchase price?

Expensive items like cars and clothes do not appreciate in value. They depreciate. They will be worth less tomorrow than

---

1   Thorstein Veblen. *Theory of the Leisure Class: An Economic Study in the Evolution of Institutions.* (New York: Macmillan, 1899), 400.

what they require of you today. You can't maximize the future value by putting your money into depreciating items. When you invest today in items that increase in value, you can create value in the future. Having a "then what?" moment can save you a lot of trouble and money!

The future value is the most important number because, I propose, delayed gratification is worth the sacrifice of investing today. In thinking about the future value, ask yourself: "Where do I want to be?" and "How do I plan to get there?"

CHAPTER FOUR: THE PRESENT VALUE

PV = present value

The present value is the amount you are willing to invest today. From now on, I will refer to this amount as your *initial investment*. The present value can be measured in any unit— dollars, minutes, compact discs, and so forth. It is merely the amount of something you are willing to sacrifice today in order to receive more of that something in the future.

Every opportunity requires some kind of investment, whether voluntary or involuntary, present or future. The earlier you invest, the better your return will be later. I am going to return to math to show you why.

Let's stick with the one thousand dollars from our previous example. This time let's see what would happen if you saved the money for a far-away future goal, like retirement. Let's leave the money in an account for thirty years at 5 percent. How much will you have at the end of thirty years?

$1,000 \text{ x } (1.05)^{30} = 1,000 \text{ x } 4.32194 = \$4,321.94$

Now, let's suppose that you waited five years to invest that $1,000.

$1,000 \text{ x } (1.05)^{25} = 1,000 \text{ x } 3.38635 = \$3,386.35$

Delaying the investment by five years cost you $935. In dollar terms, that may not seem like much, but the future value of your retirement savings is 22 percent less. That is a big difference.

You don't have to invest right now, but the sooner you invest,

The Time Value of Life

the better. By investing early, you can invest less *now* to reach the same goal *later*. In other words, with a late start, in order to reach the same goal, you will have to sacrifice more. Sometimes we simply cannot invest today. More often than not, though, we choose not to invest today. Instead, we procrastinate.

Making Up for Lost Time

When I was three or four years old, I began taking piano lessons. My teacher was a distinguished older woman named Dr. Terry (she let me call her Mrs. Terry). I would go to Mrs. Terry's apartment every Saturday morning for voice and piano lessons. I spent most of our lessons working on the piano. I sang and played in recitals that were held in homes and churches. As I got older, I began to like ragtime and Scott Joplin's *The Entertainer.* I played it so many times that one of my father's friends called me "The Entertainer" every time he saw me. I started to get bored with the piano. I played for the church choir occasionally, but only because my mother pushed me. Eventually, I quit the piano lessons and took up other activities.

In college I joined a sorority, and each semester we would host a church service on campus. A few days before a service that I was planning, our pianist backed out. I was so disappointed. No service is complete without music. So, I decided that I would play. And play I did! As I played *Leaning on the Everlasting Arms,* it was as though no time had passed. No one knew how many years it had been since I had played the piano for an audience.

I wished that I had never stopped playing. I wished that I had listened to my mother when she told me not to quit. I wished that I had listened to Mrs. Terry when she told me that "practice makes perfect."

Six years later, I was asked to speak at a program sponsored by my church in Delaware. The program featured two vocalists, one of whom was a music teacher who grew up in the area and who was a member of the church across the street. It took me a couple of months, but I enrolled in piano and voice lessons with her. I have been playing ever since.

I can't help but think back to my younger days and wonder how far along I would be if I had never stopped practicing. Perhaps I would have majored in music, or maybe I would be touring with an orchestra. Both of these are doubtful, but my point is that if I had followed through earlier, I may have been further along, and if I had invested earlier, it would have been easier.

How would it have been easier? First of all, as a child I had plenty of time on my hands. My Saturday mornings were always free for lessons, and my days and nights were free for practice, if I so pleased. I may have had a play date here or there, but I had no job, no responsibilities, and no time-consuming tasks to work around.

With a late start, in order to reach the same goal, you will have to sacrifice more.

Currently, I have set my music lesson for every Thursday, but as a grown-up, appointments can be more difficult for me to keep. I have a job, and sometimes I have more than one job. When teaching, I typically carry a load of four classes each semester. I have papers to grade and lectures to plan. I run one non-profit organization and sit on the board of another. I am sometimes called to appear on the nightly news. Other times I am asked to speak at community functions or at other universities. Add family, friends, and a social life, and things can be pretty hectic.

Secondly, I bear the cost. My current music teacher is probably the best bargain I have ever come across, but now *I* am responsible for my tuition, not my mom and dad. But, believe me, the time is much more difficult to come up with than the money.

I thought about all of the times when I said, "This is boring.

I don't feel like practicing." Now, I am enjoying myself, and I look forward to finding the time to practice.

One of the happiest memories of piano playing I have is from a recent visit with my grandmother. Grandma came to stay at my parents' house for a week, and she asked me to play the piano. I played several songs from an old hymn book and once we got to the patriotic hymns, Grandma started to sing along. She sang every verse of *My Country 'Tis of Thee, God Bless America,* and *America the Beautiful.* My dad jokingly asked us to quit it, and after we did, I laughed until I cried.

Some people look back on things like this and say, "Can you imagine what I could have been if I had done ___?" If you begin investing now, you may still be able to become whatever that blank is for you. The path may have been easier if you had started earlier, but it is still possible. Look at me. As a child, conditions were easier for me to learn and practice, but the desire to invest just wasn't there. As an adult, the desire to invest my time is there, but conditions often preclude me from learning and practicing as much as I want.

Either way, I wanted to play the piano and now I do. I am a firm believer that everything happens for a reason. As such, I am exactly where I am supposed to be in terms of my piano skills and everything else.

I have put off other things, including this book! I worked on this book for three years. I scribbled here and there, and told a few people about my ideas, but didn't really do much. Sure, I wanted to finish writing the book and eventually get it published, but I just wasn't getting any work done. In fact, the bulk of the work was done over a span of two weeks when I stopped talking about investing in it and chose to start actually investing.

Do you have a goal in mind and find yourself reluctant to invest? Look at what you want and ask yourself: "What am I willing to sacrifice? What am I waiting for?"

CHAPTER FIVE: RATE OF RETURN

r = rate of return

The rate of return is the amount you earn on your investment every period. The rate of return is expressed as a percentage, similar to an interest rate.

The rate of return is a direct measure of the risk associated with your investment. Very risky investments should have higher rates of return, and not-so risky investments should have lower rates of return. This relationship is very important, so remember two things:

1. Risk and return are directly related.
2. "r" is the only variable that can be positive or negative.

Low Risk Leads to Low Return

Let's begin the discussion of risk and reward with the most conservative investment available—a U.S. Treasury bill. A "T-bill" is a short-term bond issued by the United States Treasury Department. T-bills mature in less than one year and are backed by the full faith and credit of the U.S. government. The rate of return on a T-bill is usually small relative to rates paid on other types of investments. T-bills are sold at a discount to their face value, and interest is paid in one installment when the bills mature. I looked at the historical rates for three-month T-bills, and since 1954, the rate has ranged from 0 percent in December 2008 to just above 17 percent in December of 1980.

In December of 1980, the average rate of return on a T-bill was 15.49 percent.[2]

Using this rate, if you had purchased a $1,000 T-bill in December of 1980, the government would have paid you $134.12 of interest at the end of three months.

$$FV = PV(1 + r)^t$$

$$1,000 = PV(1+.1549)^1$$
$$PV = \$865.88$$
$$\text{Interest} = FV - PV = \$134.12$$

If you had purchased a $1,000 T-bill in November of 2008, the government would have paid you $14.78 of interest at the end of three months.

$$FV = PV(1 + r)^t$$

$$1,000 = PV(1+.015)^1$$
$$PV = \$985.22$$
$$\text{Interest} = FV - PV = \$14.78$$

There is a big difference between $14.78 and $134.12 worth of interest, but the reward for bearing risk varies every day, and rates of return should be viewed relatively.

In 1980, T-bill rates were much higher than in 2008, but inflation was much higher too. When prices rise, each dollar that you have will buy you less. The decreased purchasing power is a result of inflation. Inflation eats away at your dollars, and it can eat away at the returns on your investments. In December 1980, the average rate of return offered by a T-bill was 15.49 percent, but in the same year inflation reached 18 percent. So,

---

2   Data from the Federal Reserve Statistical Release, http://www. federalreserve.gov/releases/h15/data/Business_day/H15_TB_M3.txt, January 23, 2009.

even if you walked away with $134.12 in interest, you would not have $134.12 worth of purchasing power. All other things being equal, your dollars will buy you less in periods of higher inflation than in periods of lower inflation.

The government has yet to default on any of its debts; therefore, T-bills are often viewed as risk-free securities. Regardless of the range of rates promised over time, the government has made good on those promises. No other entity carries the same clout.

High Risk Leads to High Return

The U.S. government is the only issuer of securities that are regarded as risk-free. Securities issued by other entities, like municipalities and public companies, do not carry the same guarantee.

Public companies can issue bonds and stock. Stock is viewed as the more risky of the two securities. A share of stock represents an ownership stake in the company, and as a shareholder, you can share in a company's profits and losses. The Standard & Poor's 500 is a stock index that tracks the value of 500 large primarily U.S. companies. Many people look at indexes like the Dow Jones Industrial Average (DJIA) and the S&P 500 as indicators of domestic economic conditions.

In 1980, the S&P 500 had a 25.77 percent rate of return.[3] In 2008, the S&P 500 lost 38.49 percent of its value.[4] From this example, you can easily see that an investment in the stock market can end up as a losing investment. An investment in a bond is like an IOU that promises a stated rate of interest. An investment in a stock comes with the promise of nothing,

---

3   Historical Prices obtained from Yahoo! Finance http://finance.yahoo. com/q/hp?s=%5EGSPC&a=11&b=31&c=1979&d=11&e=31&f=1980&g= d&z=66&y=0

4   Historical Prices obtained from Yahoo! Finance http://finance.yahoo. com/q/hp?s=%5EGSPC&a=11&b=31&c=2007&d=11&e=31&f=2008&g= d&z=66&y=0

as there are no guaranteed returns. If you buy stock, you are taking a chance on the company. When times are good you may profit, and when times are bad you may lose. In the worst case scenario, you could lose everything you invest.

The wide range of returns offered by stocks is a direct result of this elevated level of risk. If an investment has a high level of risk, it should have a higher rate of return, but here's the catch: actual returns can be highly positive or highly negative.

If an opportunity offers a large reward and requires little or no investment, something is wrong.

I have been approached by people offering risky investments. These vendors say things like, "If this works, you can double your money." The question I always asked was, "What if it doesn't work?"

We saw this with the recent falling of the S&P 500 stock index, and you can see non-monetary examples in your everyday life. In real-life situations, risk and returns are difficult to quantify, but judging the risk of an investment comes down to a few common-sense points.

If an opportunity offers a large reward and requires little or no investment, something is wrong. There are many ways to generate high returns with little investment of time or money. However, I would avoid them because they are probably illegal or at least extremely risky.

I have been approached many times in my life to join "clubs" that simply sounded too good to be true. The programs ask you to donate one hundred dollars, and even though there is no promise of a gain, the literature tells you it is possible to receive fifty times your donation again and again. I have declined every invitation, and the Better Business Bureau later exposed one scenario as a pyramid scheme. Who knows how many people have lost money on schemes like this and how many others gained at the expense of those who lost.

If someone asks you for one hundred dollars and offers or promises to give you two-thousand dollars in return, you need to ask some serious questions or be like me: Save yourself some time by turning around and running the other way!

On a more serious note, sometimes an option will present itself in life that ultimately costs you more than money and more than you invested. A few years back I talked to a student—let's call him Mark—who was very bright. In my interactions with him, he always asked questions that were far deeper than those posed by his peers.

One day, as I was leaving a class, we talked about what he would do after graduation and during graduate school. I took the opportunity to tell him how important it was to be consistent with attendance and performance. I felt good after our conversation because I thought I had gotten through to him. Mark didn't come around during the following week. A few days later, I saw a headline on the Internet about a crime that took place over the weekend. I subsequently discovered that Mark was a suspect involved in the incident. Thankfully, no one was seriously hurt, but sadly, the lives of all who were involved have been changed forever. In just a few minutes, Mark changed the course of the rest of his life. This leads me to my next common-sense point.

If You Can Lose More than Your Initial Investment, "r" Is Too High

In the short term, Mark's actions cost him his degree and his freedom. After prison, they will continue to cost him for the rest of his life. With a criminal record, it will be more difficult for him to get a job. If he does get a job, it probably won't compare to the job he could have had if he had not committed the crime. In some states, he will never be able to vote or run for public office. There are too many potential consequences for me to name. These kinds of losses are immeasurable.

If a legitimate investment goes wrong, the most you can lose is what you invested.

When evaluating risk, ask yourself: "How much is too much?" Will you be comfortable with the range of possibilities?

CHAPTER SIX: TIME

t = time

The time is the number of time periods over which you plan to invest. Time can be denominated in years, months, days, or whatever time frame is relevant to your investment. Note: Interest rates must be quoted in the same time frame as "t." If your decision is based on months, your interest rate should be a monthly rate.

I usually stay up pretty late, and because of this, I have seen my fair share of infomercials, most of which revolve around weight loss or financial markets.

"Take this pill and you will lose ten pounds in two weeks ..." they advertise.

"Order this trading software and you can make your salary in one month!"

It sounds too good to be true. And guess what? It is.

Some of the most popular books are about losing weight and getting rich. Tack the word "quickly" on to either of those topics, and you've got yourself a best seller. This is something that, for the life of me, I just don't understand. If you have chosen either of these goals for yourself, get a pen and a pad. I am about to save you some time and money.

If you want to lose weight, follow the FDA's caloric recommendations and the food pyramid and exercise regularly. If you want to get rich, work intelligently and invest in things you believe in. If your goal is to do either of these things quickly, be prepared to be disappointed. The problem with so many of us is that we want the best possible outcome with the least possible investment. Does this really make sense?

When it comes to rapidly getting rich, people often point to the stock market. There is some truth in being able to reap swift rewards there, but, given my background, you know I must ask you to delve more deeply into that possibility. If you happened to have some money, and you happened to pick and purchase a stock right before it happened to have a huge return, and you happened to sell that stock before the price went back down, then, yes, you could get rich very quickly. The chances of this happening quickly and repeatedly, however, are slim to none.

Furthermore, if there were a person capable of duplicating this feat, what on earth would prompt her to share her secret with you? Once the so-called secret is out and used by others, it alters the future performance of the stock, thereby eliminating the effectiveness of the secret.

This notion of instant gratification makes me think of the microwave. The microwave is one of the greatest inventions of the twentieth century, but in my opinion, it is both a blessing and a curse. On the positive side, it cooks food speedily. After all, who feels like waiting twenty minutes to use the oven to reheat a biscuit? However, the time you save by using a microwave comes by sacrificing some of the quality of the taste and texture of the food.

With some investments, it will just take longer than others for you to see a profit.

Fast and Safe—Investing in a CD

A quick and relatively easy way to make safe returns is to visit your local bank and invest in a certificate of deposit (CD). A CD is a low-risk, short-term investment that pays interest in one installment.

Gradual and Risky—Entrepreneurship

A lengthier and more risky alternative investment would be to open your own business. If it is successful, the returns can be large, even though they will not come immediately.

Let's suppose you are a pizza lover and you decide to open your own pizzeria. Making a pizza can require many ingredients. Opening a pizzeria requires many more. Cooking will be the easiest thing you have to do!

You will need to buy or rent a physical location to house the business. You will need to furnish the location and purchase equipment such as ovens and refrigerators. You will have to pay for insurance. You will have to pay for permits and licenses, and possibly the services of accountants, lawyers, or other experts. You will need to hire employees. If you offer benefits, you will have to pay a plan administrator. You may have to pay a company to process payments for your vendors and employees. On opening day, you will need cash to make change. If you decide to accept credit and debit cards, you will have to pay merchant fees. Finally, you will need to purchase all of the ingredients necessary to make pizzas.

Let's suppose your initial investment in the pizzeria is seventy-five thousand dollars. If you expect to profit four thousand dollars each month, you will not recover your initial investment within one year of operating. Ignoring the time value of money, you would break even in a little less than nineteen months.

Does this seem like a long time? The average person lives well into his seventies, so is nineteen months really that big of a deal, especially when you have successfully opened your own business and managed to turn a profit?

Sometimes our returns come in pieces over lengthy periods of time. Let's assume you placed your monthly profits in a mutual fund that paid 7 percent per year.

The following timeline uses months to reflect the four-thousand-per-month investment. The annual interest rate of 7 percent had to be converted to a monthly interest rate (7 percent per year divided by twelve months per year = 0.583 percent).

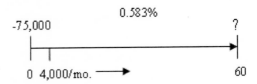

At the end of five years, you would have over $286,000 and you would have recovered your initial investment. Reaching that goal may not be easy or quick, but it is indeed possible. After all, if it weren't possible, how could there be so many pizzerias?

When you invest a substantial amount of money, it may take a long time to reap the benefits. Sometimes the benefits will come back to you in small increments.

In the realm of money, an investment that pays you back in equal, periodic increments is known as an annuity. Annuities pay you the same amount of money per period over a set amount of time.

Large jackpots usually give you the option of receiving a lump sum or an annuity. If you are familiar with any of the multi-state lotteries, examine the payment options for the grand prize. The annuity is usually paid out over thirty years. Let's suppose the jackpot was $90 million. Ninety million dollars is actually the value of the thirty-year annuity. So, if you opted for the annuity, you would receive thirty annual payments. Each payment would be one-thirtieth of the jackpot, which would be three million dollars in this case.

On the other hand, if you chose the lump sum, the value of the jackpot would drop somewhere in the neighborhood of 50 percent. So, perhaps you would receive a one-time payment of forty-five million dollars.

Why the huge gap? The Time Value of Money! Lottery officials know that money you have today is more valuable than the promise of money each year for the next thirty years. Using whatever their relevant rate of interest is, they determine the present value of thirty annual payments of three million dollars.

In the first case, you would physically collect ninety million dollars, but you wouldn't have ninety million dollars worth of purchasing power, since the cash flows would be spread over thirty years. In the second case, you would have forty-five million dollars today and the freedom to spend or invest it right now. Depending on interest rates, the forty-five million may be the best deal. Annuities can be good because they encourage patterned behavior, but when choosing between a lump sum and an annuity, do the math first.

CHAPTER SEVEN: THE TIME VALUE OF LIFE

In the business world, the future value is based strictly upon cash flows. Future cash flows must be weighed against the required investment to determine if a project will be profitable.

Before accepting a project, business owners estimate how much money they will invest in the project and how much money they expect to receive from the project. Since they will spend cash today and receive cash in the future, they must recognize that the expectation of future dollars will not be worth as much as the receipt of dollars today. They examine the project's risk in order to determine an appropriate interest rate. Then, the Time Value of Money (TVM) model is used to solve for the present value of the expected cash flows.

In order to determine if an investment is truly worthwhile, each future cash flow must be discounted (using the time value of money) and treated as if it were occurring today.

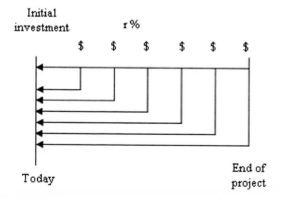

Each expected cash flow is a future value. We must solve for the present value of each cash flow. The sum of these inflows must be greater than the initial investment.

The discounted future cash flows are then added together and the sum is compared to the initial investment. The difference between the two is referred to as the Net Present Value (NPV).

The NPV equals:

$$\sum_{n=1}^{t} \frac{\text{Future cash flow at "t"}}{(1+r)^{t}} - PV$$

Why is it called the net present value? Each project is evaluated as if the costs and benefits all occurred at one point—today. The "net" is the difference between those values in today's terms.

Generally speaking, businesses do not want to take on projects that will set them back. The decision rule is that if the NPV is greater than zero, a project is acceptable. If the NPV is less than zero, the project is unacceptable.

Sometimes companies have projects with negative NPVs. This is commonly found with research and development projects. Sometimes you have to spend money in order to figure out if something works, such as a new machine or medicine. Still, the goal of a business is to maximize the value for its owners. The best way to achieve this goal is to accept projects that create value by way of a high net present value.

Time Value of Life as a Decision-Making Tool for Life

The premise of the Time Value of Money (TVM) model is so basic that it can be used to evaluate any kind of situation, financial or otherwise.

My adaptation of TVM can be applied to everyday life decisions through what I call the Time Value of Life (TVL).

Every moment of our lives has value; and just like TVM, we control the value by controlling the inputs.

With TVL, gains do not have to be made of money. They could be made of knowledge, experience, or whatever is important enough to you to make your investment worthwhile.

I can tell you some things that are important to me (in no particular order): my faith, my family, my community, my contribution to society, my time, and my health. Knowing that these things are important to me makes me think of them when I make decisions regarding my time.

FV should always be greater than PV. If PV is ever greater than FV, then you have made a bad investment.

When I contemplate how to invest my time, I have to ask myself questions such as:

If I do this, will it aid my family?

If I do that, will it aid my community?

Unlike TVM, with life I can't always tell how much value my investments will create, but this is the formula that I need to satisfy:

Future Value > Present Value

With TVL, you don't need numbers. All you need to do is learn how to invest your time, and the goal is simple: maximize the future value.

In other words, FV should always be greater than PV. If PV is ever greater than FV, then you have made a bad investment. When FV is greater than PV, you have made a good investment.

The difference between FV and PV is the reward you earn for investing.

Therefore:

FV = PV + gains

A profitable investment will maximize your gains. The best investment will provide adequate gains for the level of risk assumed.

A good investment of time will bring you rewards far greater than you could imagine. Time well invested can lead to value far greater than a monetary investment ever could.

There are many ways to maximize your future value. If we look at the TVM formula inputs, here are your options:

1. Increase PV
2. Increase t
3. Increase r

This translates to:

1. Make a larger initial investment.
2. Make a lengthy commitment to your investment.
3. Make a more risky investment.

All three actions will raise the future value, but one of them has the potential to backfire. High risk investments can go both ways because "r" is the only factor that can be positive or negative. Remember the S&P 500?

If all of the variables are positive, your future value will be greater than the present value. So, the only way to make a profitable investment is to have all positive inputs.

This means that the value of your future comes down to time and sacrifice. The most desirable outcome for any investment is for your future value to be greater than the value of your initial investment. You may not be able to accurately estimate all of the

> *The value of your future comes down to time and sacrifice.*

benefits. Sometimes, you may not even estimate the costs correctly.

The key to the Time Value of Life is forethought. Even if your estimates turn out to be wrong, you can at least think through enough to weigh the costs and benefits before acting. We control the use of the most precious resource available to us—time. Time is a valuable and limited resource; we should be careful how we use it!

Life often presents us with difficult decisions regarding our time and money. The following chapters highlight some investing tips that I use when considering what to do with my resources. Each tip comes with a business-world lesson, after which you will find some of my personal experiences with time, value, and life.

CHAPTER EIGHT: RECOGNIZE A LIMITED RESOURCE

What would happen if the United States ran out of money?

I will never say that anything is impossible, but this one is a long shot. If, for some reason, the country ran out of dollars, the mint could just print more. Another alternative would be to use something other than dollars as currency. Perhaps a new currency would be created.

I read recently about a city that has decided to print its own money. This is not a far-fetched idea; in fact, there are several towns that have their own currency. I liken this to special tokens for the subway in certain cities or tickets at the carnival.

Running out of dollars may be unlikely, but the dollar can run out of value.

On November 19, 2008, one U.S. dollar was worth 1.2294 Canadian dollars (CAD). In Japan, the U.S. dollar was worth 96.61898 yen (JPY). Four months earlier, one U.S. dollar was worth 1.00103 CAD or 105.422 JPY.[5] In different parts of the world, and even different parts of this country, your dollars may not be worth as much as they are in your hometown.

The falling value of a dollar can be detrimental to those of us who use dollars daily, but it can help others. Currency trading allows people to bet on the value of money. You could have a U.S. dollar or an Indian rupee today, and tomorrow both of their values could be totally different.

Ten years ago, a dollar could have bought you two cans of soda. Perhaps today it is only worth one. Even if the country didn't run out of money, a dollar could be worthless tomorrow, and there is little if anything that we could do about it. It doesn't matter where you are in the world—in Canada, China, or the

5   Data obtained from the FXConverter at www.oanda.com

U.S. A minute is always a minute and an hour is always an hour. When I go to sleep, someone on the other side of the world is waking up, but they will count their hours just like I count mine.

When Time Runs Out: Awakening from the Dream

In the past, I have put off many things in my life because I never thought about not being able to accomplish those things at a future date. I assumed that there would always be a moment when I could complete them—later. I don't make that assumption anymore. Now I know that time is a limited resource. Now that the dreams have become reality, I know that time runs out.

On the Wednesday after the dreams began, I saw someone looking in Michael's car as I was walking to choir rehearsal. So, out of concern for his safety (I was actually concerned about the car), I called him. He was visiting a friend who lived about a block from my church. I told him about my concern, and he told me that I was an angel, floating around helping people on earth. I laughed and he told me that he was going to come over with a calendar and let me pick the dates for the surprise trip, since I was such a busybody. I smiled and agreed. He told me that he also would bring some Nathan's brand hot dogs (my favorite!). I laughed and he said, "Okay, I'll give you a call later." I told him I would talk to him later and I headed into the church with a huge smile on my face.

The next night, I put on a sweatshirt that he had given me for Christmas, said my prayers, and went to sleep.

It was hard for me to sleep because I had finally gotten up the nerve to tell the other man that it was over. I had felt so relieved after telling him. We both had known it was coming. I figured I would take a couple of weeks to myself, plan the trip, and see what happened next.

I woke up the next morning and went to work. I was a little

40

nervous, because I had to give a speech after class and I had nothing to wear. I went to the mall on my lunch break, bought a basic, white button-down shirt and a pair of khakis, and returned to campus. On the way back to my office, I noticed a fire truck and ambulance behind me, and I wondered what had happened. Before I could pull over, both vehicles turned onto the street I had just passed. The meter-maid who normally issued parking tickets was standing on the corner directing traffic away from that street.

During class, I went online and saw that there had been an accident and that a man had been killed. I talked to my students and even some other faculty members about it. I said a prayer for the person's family and instructed others to do the same.

After work, I went home to quickly change for the speech. I saw some news coverage of the accident on television and my home phone was ringing. Then my cell phone rang. I was in a rush, so I left the house and returned the call from my car.

It was Michael's aunt. She sounded shaken and asked me to come to her house right away. I kept questioning why. She asked, "Did you hear about the accident?"

Of course I had heard about it. I drove by it. Someone was killed.

Then she told me it was him. The accident had killed a person and it was Michael.

I kept driving, replaying her words in my mind. I tried to breathe deeply, but breathing became hard. I held it together for about a mile. At the next light, I screamed and cried for a few seconds, which seemed like an eternity. When the light turned green, I snapped back and thought about what I had to do next.

Each of us controls the value of the minutes and hours we are given.

The building where I was supposed to give the speech was located on campus, on the way to Michael's family's house. I wiped my eyes and drove to campus. The student who had recommended me for the speech was waiting outside. She located the person in charge of the program, and I told him what had happened and that I had to go to the family. The house was about a mile away, but the drive seemed so long. My eyes were stinging and my vision was blurry from all of the tears.

I pulled into Michael's aunt's driveway to find police officers, one male and one female, waiting for me. They asked me for my name. They told me that shortly after noon that day Michael had died. I realized then that the fire truck and ambulance that had been behind me had been trying to get to him.

I will never be able to fully put into words the pain that I felt. It felt like somebody was squeezing my heart, and just as my knees were about to buckle, the person would let go, over and over again.

Much of what happened next was a blur of phone calls, text messages, and people coming into and out of the house. I drove to the church to get chairs for the visitors. I went to the scene of the accident. I went to the police station to find out how I could get his personal effects from the medical examiner's office. I went to the towing yard to find his car.

My mother and sister arrived later that night. We took his little sister with us to stay in a hotel. I left the room several times that night to go to the lobby. I sat down at a table and cried. I used the hotel computer to read old e-mails he had sent me. I went into the bathroom and cried. I probably would have spent the night in that lobby, if not for the presence of some annoying, tiny ants crawling all over the floor.

That night I couldn't sleep because I just couldn't stop thinking. *"This can't be happening. We were supposed to have more time."*

I have always thought about what might have happened if I had hugged him that day, or if I had left the other relationship earlier.

A lot of people said things like, if I had done something—a phone call, a text message, or anything to alter the course of that day—maybe the outcome would have been different. Maybe he'd still be here.

My Grandma Lucille often says, "You can't take a trip on a horse named 'If.'"

So, I have set the "ifs" aside because I cannot change the past. I miss him, but I have no regrets. If I did, I would be giving myself far too much credit, far too much power to change the course of the world. Instead, I face the future, without assuming that there will be more time.

Each of us controls the value of the minutes and hours we are given. There can always be more money, but time can never be replaced.

CHAPTER NINE: REINVESTMENT

Have you ever thought that once you got that one thing, your life would be complete?

When you receive dividends, you can keep the cash or you can buy more stock in the company. If you choose to buy more stock, you have decided to reinvest.

When it comes to the world of investment management, there is constant pressure to make more money and earn higher returns. The two most basic types of investments used are bonds and stocks. Asset managers must decide how much they want to place in each.

Both have different risks and benefits. With stocks there are no guarantees, since the value of stock fluctuates. If you purchase stock, you can make money when the stock price rises or if the stock pays dividends. A dividend is a payment from a company to its stockholders. Companies pay dividends after they decide to share a portion of their profits with the owners. Dividends are optional and can be adjusted or stopped at anytime.

The graphic below shows the cash flows associated with a dividend paying stock.

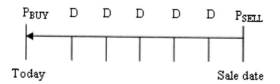

Each "D" represents a dividend payment. When investing in stock, you would like to end with more than you started.

$$P_{SELL} - P_{BUY} + Dividends = Profit \text{ or } Loss$$

When you receive dividends, you can keep the cash, or you can buy more stock in the company. If you choose to buy more stock, you have decided to reinvest. Your broker will take your dividends and buy you more shares of the company's stock. By putting the cash back into the company, you can make more money in the future.

Things are different with bonds, since a bond represents a legally binding IOU. You know exactly how much you will collect in the future as soon as you buy the bond. A long-term bond will provide periodic interest payments at a predetermined rate and one large payment at maturity.

Let me explain. Most lenders do not like to lend their money for long periods of time, but most borrowers want loans that they can pay back over long periods of time. To compromise, a borrower makes small payments to the lender throughout the life of a loan and makes one large payment when the loan expires.

For example, if you buy an eight-year $10,000 bond from Kal-Mart, you wouldn't want to wait eight years to collect your $10,000 plus interest. Kal-Mart will pay you interest periodically (usually once or twice per year) for eight years, and in the last year, give you $10,000.

Let's say that your interest payment arrives once per year and is 5 percent of the bond's value. So each year you will collect .05 x $10,000 = $500. Once you receive this money, you can spend it or you can reinvest it in something else.

If you choose to reinvest, there is a risk that you may not be able to earn as high a return as your previous investment. This is called reinvestment rate risk. Perhaps after you buy your bond from Kal-Mart, the going rate on bonds falls to 4 percent.

Sure, 4 percent is less than 5 percent, but if you spend the money, as opposed to reinvesting it, you won't earn anything.

In most cases, receiving the benefit of this bond would not be enough to satisfy an investor. Investors would like to see continuous returns or a pattern that maintains what they have received in the past.

Real-Life Reinvesting

"Once I buy a house, I will be just fine."
"Once I lose ten pounds, I will be perfect."
"Once I get that job, I will be set!"

The fallacy of each of these statements is that the attainment of the item is not the end. It is just the beginning.

I remember moving from an apartment to a house. It was a big step—what I called a grown-up move. Buying a home required additional investments after I completed the purchase. Now I have to maintain its appearance and its suitability for my needs. Because I have a yard, I have to cut the grass, and I've even done some landscaping. I have cleaned the gutters, raked leaves in the fall, and shoveled snow in the winter. This is all in addition to the dusting, mopping, vacuuming, and other regular cleaning duties. There is more space to furnish and therefore more space and furniture to clean.

No longer will a condo association take care of the grass and landscaping in the summer, or plow the snow during winter. No more calling the landlord to take care of every problem. I closed on my house less than thirty days after making the offer, but I might live in this house for the rest of my life. So, I can't be content with just being the owner!

Instead of saying, "Once I buy a house, I will be just fine," you should say, "Once I buy a house, I will be a homeowner. I must continually reinvest time, energy, and even more dollars into my home if I want to retain its value."

When I lost that ten pounds (in my case it was closer to forty, but I'll have to explain that in another book!), it didn't come off from the places I wanted it to. I have been teased since childhood about my weight. As a kid, I was called "lollipop" because my head was big and I was skinny. As an adolescent, I had a growth spurt and was teased because I had a big bottom. After my freshman year of high school, I started working out regularly and lost forty pounds, but my legs were still big! When I went shopping for suits, I had to buy small tops and medium bottoms. I remember going to buy a suit in college and I had to get a size seven jacket and size eleven pants. To this day, people tell me about my legs. As an adult, I don't care about the comments, but as a young lady, those types of insults were hard for me to brush off.

Healthy weight loss can be a difficult but rewarding process. Studies show that weight regains are most likely in the first couple of years after weight loss. "The recent estimates are that 5 percent to 10 percent of people are successful at keeping weight off on a long-term basis," says Paul MacLean, associate professor of medicine at the University of Colorado, Denver.[6]

Think about your "diet": What will you do once it is over? You could go out and eat all of the foods you had to avoid in order to lose the weight. You could stop working out as much because, if you are like me, you never really liked working out anyway.

There is no way to keep the weight off without working to do so. If you return to your old habits, you will most certainly return to your old weight. Again, you must continually invest time and energy, and you must continually sacrifice your momentary appetite, in order to retain your weight loss.

Let's revisit the example about saving for your child's college education. If you invest $10,000 up front and need $70,000 in fifteen years, you will need an investment that consistently pays an annual return of 13.85 percent. The odds of finding something like this are slim to none.

---

6   Shari Roan. "Why It's Hard to Maintain Weight Loss." *Los Angeles Times*, 2 June 2008.

Let's see what will happen if you invest the $10,000 today and continue to invest a smaller amount, $1,000 each year, until your child turns eighteen.

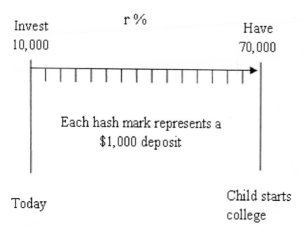

We have two types of cash flows here: a lump-sum investment of $10,000 and a fifteen year annuity of $1,000.
Here's the formula:

FV = FV lump sum + FV annuity = $70,000
The future value of the lump sum = $PV(1 + r)^t$

The future value of the annuity takes more work
FV = $[((1+r)^{15} - 1)/r]$ x 1,000

$70,000 = $10,000$(1 + r)^{15}$ + $[((1+r)^{15} - 1)/r]$ x 1,000

Now you can see why I recommended the calculator! The interest rate required to meet the goal has now dropped to 9.55 percent. The lower interest rate means that you can take on less risk. This is still a lofty rate to expect consistently from any investment. The only ways to further reduce risk and still attain your goals are to either invest more money, or start investing earlier, or both.

Maintenance

The reinvestment process doesn't end just because you reach your goal. It simply shifts gears. The next gear is called maintenance, and it is a form of reinvesting.

When I got "that" car, I didn't properly estimate how much it would cost to maintain. In my online car search, I neglected to look for what grade of gasoline the car required. After buying the car and opening up the fuel door, I discovered that premium gasoline was recommended. I had no way of knowing that gas would rise above four dollars per gallon, and that the car would soon begin to make a squeaking noise that three trips to the dealer and one trip to an independent mechanic would fail to resolve.

Once I got "that" job, I didn't realize how much of my free time would be overtaken by work. For me, that job was returning to my alma mater to teach in the Finance Department. I taught full-time for one semester and absolutely loved it. After the semester ended, I took a job at a big bank and spent most of my tenure there trying to find a way back into the classroom. After one year of being overqualified and undercompensated, I returned to teaching. I looked at the pros of my exit from big business. No more nine-to-five days. I only had to teach three days a week. I had my own office instead of a wide open cubicle. I decided what to teach instead of someone telling me what to do. I had every major holiday off, plus summers and winter breaks! Fabulous!

The grass can be greener on your side of the fence if you water it.

There were drawbacks, however. I would have more than 150 students and there was just one me. I'd have to repeat myself with the same level of depth and enthusiasm four times a day. I'd have students calling or e-mailing me at all types of crazy hours. I would be solely responsible for grading exams every three to four weeks. I had to make a lot of copies, and put together lectures, exams, and lesson plans.

Something I did not account for was continuing education. Each semester some new, hot topic emerged in the world of money—the rise and fall of Enron, scheming executives going to prison, the credit crunch, and the subprime mortgage meltdown. Believe me, I didn't get paid enough to stay on top of all of that, but it never stopped students from asking. I spent many of my office hours researching current events and trying to incorporate them into my lessons. I didn't have to do this, but I wanted my students to have a balance of reality and book knowledge, because I had learned that the textbook stuff didn't really prepare me for the real world.

In fast times like these, it is easy to become outdated and complacent, so we all have to do maintenance in our chosen work fields.

We are all guilty of placing our "everything" on the attainment of one thing. Getting that car, losing that weight, or getting the new job can all be satisfying accomplishments, but life afterwards will not be perfect just because you meet these goals.

To modify an old expression, I say that the grass can be greener on your side of the fence if you water it. Once you attain your goal, it is your job to maintain it!

CHAPTER TEN: DIVERSIFY YOUR INVESTMENTS

When it comes to financial markets, any good advisor will tell you never to put all of your eggs in one basket. The same applies to life.

Many people invest their retirement plan dollars in shares of their employer's stock. Let's suppose an employee, Jake, has a retirement account with $75,000 worth of his company's stock. He has been contributing to the plan for ten years. The company falls upon tough times and Jake decides to hold on to his stock. Just one year later, Jake's company files for bankruptcy protection. At the market's close on the day of the bankruptcy announcement, Jake's account is worth $365. Jake has just lost 99.5 percent of his retirement money.

What's sad in many of these cases is that the employees are kept out of the loop. You would think they would know that something is wrong, but anyone who leaves his money in the shares obviously doesn't know what is about to happen.

I worked for a publicly traded firm, and in one day, the stock lost 50 percent of its value. I had no clue that this was coming. I had been buying shares regularly and wanted to make this a long-term investment. I used some of my pay to buy shares of the stock because I believed in the company. I later read that the sell off was triggered by the company's failure to meet earnings expectations.

That company's future was short lived. Thankfully, I was already gone!

A Diversified Life

Like the financial markets, life does not guarantee that any investment will be successful. As such, we need to have multiple investments, so that if one investment goes wrong, we have another one going right to balance things out. At any point in time, we can be in the process of making multiple investments with different horizons.

> *We need to have multiple investments, so that if one investment goes wrong, we have another one going right to balance things out.*

I am an author. I am the chief executive of a non-profit. I am working on a professional certification. I am taking piano lessons. I am a daughter, a sister, and a friend. I have many more roles, and each requires a lot of work, but each benefits me in a different way.

What if I publish this book and no one buys it, and I have no Plan B? That's the question I asked myself up front. So, to keep my options open (and keep the income flowing), I took up freelance writing assignments on finance. I also continued applying for jobs, but on a much more selective basis. I have no real desire to return to corporate America, but I could return for a while and continue to work on my personal writing projects, because sometimes we have to sacrifice now in order to get what we want later.

Speaking of corporate America, knowing how to do only one thing in the job market can make you easily expendable or replaceable. One way to set yourself apart from everyone else is to gain as much knowledge as you can. Diversify your skill set. Don't get too comfortable doing just one thing. Try to improve upon that one thing or learn what the people around you are doing. You will become a more valuable part of the team.

CHAPTER ELEVEN: KEEPING YOUR WORD CREATES VALUE

A recent article on worldwide bond defaults jolted me. According to Standard & Poor's data, eighty-five companies defaulted on debts, with a combined value of $284 billion. The vast majority of the companies (seventy out of eighty-five) are in the United States.

Bonds issued by companies that may have difficulty repaying the debt are called junk bonds. They are called junk because the value placed upon the word of the issuer is next to nothing. Junk-bond investors know that there is an elevated risk they will not see any returns. In exchange for assuming the elevated risk, they demand elevated returns.

Credit default is costly and its effects are not limited to the issuing company and its bondholders.

How high is the elevated return? It depends on the company, the type of bond, and prevailing market interest rates (among other things). One way to gauge the risk and return is to look at credit spreads. Credit spreads represent the extra return investors demand for purchasing more risky bonds.

On December 1, 2008, the U.S. speculative grade bond spread had risen to 19.19 percent.[6] This represents the premium that junk bond issuers have to offer in order to attract investors.

Credit default is costly, and its effects are not limited to the issuing company and its bondholders.

Trust Has Value

Having people you can trust is a blessing. How do you determine who is trustworthy and who is not? The only way to figure this out is through trial and error. When someone makes a promise and keeps it, they build trust. The more promises they keep, the more you trust them. The word of a trustworthy person has value.

The concept of credit is similar. If you borrow something and repay it as promised, you will develop good credit. If you borrow and sometimes repay or do not repay at all, you will develop bad credit. Your credit history is maintained so that lenders can evaluate your behavior with past debts and determine how they will treat you now.

Every time you sign off on a credit card purchase, you will see some text under the signature line about the terms of repayment. I pulled a couple of receipts out of my purse and read the following statements:

"I agree to pay above total according to my card issuer agreement."

"Cardholder will pay card issuer above amount pursuant to cardholder agreement."

My signature on the line above both phrases is a symbol of my word, and my repayment of each debt shows that my word can be trusted. When I sign my name to something, it is serious business.

Would you want to make a deal with a person whose word didn't hold much weight? If you invest your time and the person defaults, there is no way to get your time back. If you make a financial investment, this shady person may not pay you back.

Likewise, if you want people to invest in you, they will want assurances that you will pay them back. Most investors will not entertain investing in you if they think it will waste their time or money. If they give you any of their time or lend you any of their money, they will expect to be better off afterwards. Why would they invest if there was a high chance that you, the borrower, could not deliver?

If you have a habit of not paying people back, you may have to search long and hard to find investors. If you do find a person or an entity that agrees to lend you the money, it will be at a very high interest rate. The fact that you are more risky forces you to compensate them for taking on your risk. If you have a credit card, read the fine print and you will see exactly what I mean. Look at your terms and you will see how quickly and drastically things change when you miss or make a late payment. Most cards charge you a late payment fee and then your interest rate changes to the "default APR" (since you defaulted on a payment).

Keeping your word creates value, because paying your debts today can save you time and money in the future.

CHAPTER TWELVE: BE RESPECTFUL OF TIME

In the previous chapter, I mentioned that several companies defaulted on interest payments for their bonds. Many of those companies opted to forego multi-million dollar interest payments in order to conserve liquidity. Missing a payment like this is damaging to a company's reputation and can make future financing more difficult and costly.

An opportunity cost is the value of the benefits you forfeit when you choose one option over another.

I imagine people who owned those bonds are angry. They may have had plans to spend their interest payments or invest them in something else. Those who planned to reinvest the money will lose twice. First, they don't get their money, and then they will miss out on any returns the reinvested money would have made.

A forgone benefit is referred to as an opportunity cost. An opportunity cost is the value of the benefits you forfeit when you choose one option over another.

In the case of the bondholders, they did not have a choice in the matter of a default. Nonetheless, they must bear the costs. Some may be more prepared to sustain a loss than others. Some people rely on bonds for income during retirement, since the cash flows are supposed to be stable.

Making late payments or skipping payments altogether is bad news for the borrower and lender. This type of behavior inconveniences the lender and hurts the borrower's chance of finding new lenders.

In the business world, suppliers will often reward their clients for paying early. If you have ever seen an invoice with the term "1% 10, net 30," this indicates that payment in full is due within thirty days and the merchant will give you a 1 percent discount if you pay the bill in full within ten days. This is proof of how much a supplier values time and money.

Respecting Time in Everyday Life

Have you ever expected a check on payday and ended up getting nothing? If this has happened to you, I'm sure you were irritated. While direct deposit has helped reduce the rate of these occurrences, I've still been shortchanged on several occasions. It happened to me once on New Year's Eve and I was really heated! I had plans for that night and those plans included my paycheck.

Have you ever gone to an event that started an hour or so later than scheduled? I have been to—and participated in—a few weddings that ended up like this. These days, when it comes to weddings, I know now just to write off the whole day. Before I adopted this policy, I tried to budget my time around a wedding. In my mind, my schedule may have looked like this:

Wedding	12 noon
Ceremony ends (at the latest)	1:15
Reception starts by	2:30
I can leave by	4:00
Be home by	4:30
Regroup and go to a movie at	6:30

If the wedding started an hour late, then my mental schedule went awry. Other unexpected delays would push back, or, in the worst case, negate my plans for the evening. I don't think people intentionally run behind schedule, but regardless of their intent, they may adversely affect my plans.

When others do not respect your time, it can be costly. The

more time you spend on their activities, the less time you have available to spend elsewhere doing something you want or have to do. This is another example of opportunity costs—the time you forfeited in order to benefit the activities of another person.

If you want respect, you should be respectful. This statement holds true in and out of time.

I have a habit of arriving at appointments just in the nick of time or a few minutes late. Recently, I held true to form on a day when I had a doctor's appointment. My sister called me about two hours before I was set to wake up. Then I tried to go back to sleep and she called me two more times. I was sluggish up until the thirty-minute mark when I began to rush. Thankfully, there was no traffic. I made it to the front desk in my doctor's office by 10:53 AM. Unfortunately, my appointment had been scheduled for eight minutes earlier. I was called in around 11:15 and I had to wait a few more minutes before the doctor came to see me. I wasn't angry. The delay made perfect sense. I didn't keep my appointment, so how could I expect him to see me immediately? By not keeping my appointment, I had thrown off his schedule, and I couldn't hold anyone else responsible. He had other patients and a few drug representatives to see. He may have assumed that I was a no-show and decided to proceed with the rest of his day.

Keep your appointments or let someone know in advance if you cannot keep them. I am still a work in progress on this one, but the point is this: if you want respect, you should be respectful. This statement holds true in and out of time.

CHAPTER THIRTEEN: BELIEVE IN YOUR INVESTMENTS

A Federal Reserve Board survey taken in 1948 showed that 90 percent of adults opposed buying stocks.[7] Primary reasons for this opposition were belief that stocks were unsafe and lack of knowledge. I can't blame anyone for questioning the safety of stocks, but lack of knowledge in this area can be remedied.

I am certain that it would have taken much more work for the average person to learn about stocks in 1948, but there is currently no excuse for being without stock market knowledge. I remember a time when I had to actually go to the library and check out books on finance. With the advance of the Internet, I can now obtain knowledge on stocks without leaving my home, and there are television channels totally devoted to financial markets.

> *If you don't understand it and can't figure it out, then you probably shouldn't invest in it.*

Many people think it is easy for financial professionals to provide specific investment advice, such as picking stocks. No one has a perfect track record. In fact, most professional money managers do not beat the market.

There are too many variables involved in running a company for any outside investor to know all of what's really going on. Many people on the inside never know all of what's really going on. That's why I don't give stock tips. I tell people to invest in what they believe in. If you don't understand it and can't figure it out, then you probably shouldn't invest in it.

The same applies to life. The more knowledge we have about something, the greater case we can build to believe or not believe in it.

The hardest part of getting into the stock market is placing the first trade. I think the hardest part of investing in anything is actually going through with the investment. A deeper base of knowledge may be enough to push us from talking about it to being about it!

Real-Life Belief

Can you think of someone who is constantly talking about doing something? When you see them, they are quick to tell you about something they are planning to do. You see them again and they are still in the planning phase. You may see them later and they have moved on to planning something else. Many people talk about things but never actually do them. Perhaps they doubt themselves, or they are afraid of losses or failure.

Belief in an investment represents a belief in yourself and your judgment. Investing your resources in anything shows that you have enough confidence in your beliefs to take action and assume risk. That's a big deal. Your actions may not always be able to affect the performance of an investment, but the fact that you talked the talk and then walked the walk sets you apart from the masses!

Writing this book was an exhausting process. Two weeks before I completed it, I went out with a few friends for snacks. After everyone left, I went over to my friend's house for some pre-Thanksgiving cheesecake. Over cheesecake, I told him how tired I was of living in Delaware. Everybody there knew me, and someone was always asking for something. I had met some really good people, but I met others who spread hurtful rumors about me during a very painful time in my life. I had taught almost a thousand students and it seemed as if everywhere I went there was somebody who knew me. I have been quite the social butterfly for some time, but I was growing tired of being known and always being asked to come to events and so forth. I just needed some alone time to grieve and regroup.

Anyway, I told my friend about an idea I had to move to

Florida so that I could get away and focus. He asked me how much it would cost to publish this book, and I told him I didn't know. I had visited a few self-publishing Web sites and ran the numbers for soft cover, hardback, color, and black-and-white, but I hadn't figured out any of the details. I reasoned that I would finish the book first and then make the publishing decision.

He asked if I had any investors. I said no, but told him that I have a music teacher who was editing for me. He asked me how long it would take me to finish the book. I said three to four months. I told him I was writing for other companies to help with my bills, but every minute I spent writing for them was another minute taken away from writing this book (opportunity cost). He asked me what the book was about, and I told him it was about the way people treat time and money. I told him a few of the real-life situations that I was writing about. He said he liked the idea, and then he left the living room. About a minute later, he returned with a stack of money. I declined the offer a few times, but he wouldn't take no for an answer. He put $1,000 in my purse and offered these three words: "Finish the book."

I was speechless. Have you ever had a person believe in you at a time when you had trouble believing in yourself? I couldn't think of what to say. Halfway through my thank-you speech, he gave me a hug and I broke down crying. It wasn't the money. It was the fact that he believed in me and what I was trying to do. Several people have told me, "Hey, that's a good idea," but he believed enough to invest in me. If this isn't an example of "Put your money where your mouth is," I don't know what would be!

In the business world, this type of person may be referred to as an "angel investor." They provide financial support to a start-up business with the expectation of high returns. In this case, my angel investor is closer to the non-business definition of an angel. He invested in me with the expectation of greatness, but with no questions asked about being paid back. He swore me to secrecy. I convinced him to let me tell the story, but he insisted that I not identify him. God sent me an angel investor at just the right time.

God has a way of doing that. He knows what you need and when you need it. I have tried to make things happen on my own time, only to have them happen when it was *the right time*.

Speaking of timing, I had two good friends, Lori and Dave, for whom I attempted to play matchmaker. They were acquainted in high school and Lori always said Dave was cute. So, I invited Lori over to my house and I called Dave to get him to come over. Once he arrived, the three of us talked for a little bit. Then I went into the next room to let them talk. Not long after I did so, Dave just up and left! Lori and I were dumbfounded. They were talking and getting along, and then he simply walked out. I gave up on the matchmaker scheme after that.

A few years later at our five-year high school reunion, Dave asked me about Lori. I told him, "Don't bother." At the time, she had been dating the same guy for a few years, and acted as though she couldn't even look at other men. Dave seemed optimistic and I told him again that it would be pointless to pursue Lori. He didn't listen and they exchanged numbers. The following year, Lori's relationship ended, after five years. No one saw it coming and she was devastated.

She called Dave and they began dating. She resisted his desire to be a couple for a while, but soon she committed. In August of 2004, they were married and I was one of Lori's maids of honor.

In my toast, I told the story of how I tried to hook them up and how Dave was totally oblivious. Apparently, Lori had never told him that story! Anyway, in my toast I talked about how things may not be right according to our time, and sometimes we have to wait for God's time. I told the guests that if my matchmaking efforts had succeeded back then, we would not have been gathered here today.

I have another friend who was forced, literally, to put his dream off for a short while. He had just entered his senior year of college, and I went to see him play in the football team's season opener. At halftime, I watched him run into the tunnel as a little girl ran up and reached out to him. He was the only member of the football team who stopped for her. He gave her a high five and headed for the locker room.

In the last minute of the last quarter, the opposing quarterback threw a pass to the player my friend was guarding. My friend leapt into the air and came down in an awkward way. He landed on the ground and didn't move. I watched from the end zone, terrified and on the verge of tears, waiting for him to get up.

From my angle, it looked as if he had snapped his neck. Finally, I saw him move and he was taken off the field and put on a golf cart. He left in an ambulance. I was so worried. I called one of his teammates, and he told me that the injury was bad, but he had no more details. I had just talked to my friend about the possibility of him turning professional the next year. He had pressure coming at him from all angles. His family and friends expected big things from him. He was a very good player, but our school had a very short list of players who had made it to the NFL. I knew both facts, and I told him that he was going to make it anyway. He had a work ethic and a passion for the game that I have only seen in a few people.

As soon as I heard from him, he told me that his season was over. It was his senior year and his season had been ended in the very first game. I felt so bad for him, but I told him that he would be better and stronger for the ordeal. Throughout the season I watched him on the sidelines, coaching from his crutches. He was so inspiring. I knew how much it hurt him to not be able to participate, but he put that hurt aside to help his team.

I hoped he would be granted a medical red shirt and I told

him that next year he would make captain, and after he went pro, Fox would do a *Beyond the Glory* special on him. Well, he got the medical redshirt and made a full recovery. The next year he made captain, his team won the championship, and he went on to the NFL.

Without that devastating injury, who knows if the story would have had the same ending? God knew he needed another year. As much as it hurt, I know he wouldn't have changed a thing. After he realized his dream, I sent him an e-mail to say, "I told you so."

Sometimes we need a nudge to remind us that we are worth investing in.

CHAPTER FOURTEEN: MAKE COLLABORATIVE INVESTMENTS

One way to make a collaborative investment in financial markets is through the use of mutual funds. You can buy shares in a mutual fund just as easily as you can buy shares of stock, but with lower risk. Mutual funds accept money from hundreds or thousands of investors. The money is pooled together, and then used to purchase stocks, bonds, and other securities. Here's a numerical example to show how a mutual fund can help you diversify and save money.

Suppose you have one thousand dollars and would like to invest in stocks. You like three companies: The Cake Place, Macrosoft, and Specific Electric. The stocks are currently trading at eight, twenty-two, and twenty dollars per share respectively. Your broker charges you ten dollars per trade.

For starters, you must subtract thirty dollars in broker commissions for each order to buy shares of stock in each company. After fees, you have $970 to invest.

One possible combination of the three stocks that adds up to $970 is listed below:

Fifty shares in The Cake Place at $8 per share = $400
Five shares in Macrosoft at $22 per share = $110
Twenty-three shares in Specific Electric at $20 per share = $460

If you choose to sell your shares, your proceeds will be ten dollars lower after you pay your broker for processing the trade.

Now, what if you found a mutual fund that invested in all three of these stocks? First, you would only have to pay one commission if you used a broker. With some funds, those fees can be avoided by dealing directly with the mutual fund. Second, your money would be pooled with money from other investors. This larger amount of money will allow the fund's managers to purchase a wider selection of securities than you could afford on your own. Third, access to so many securities decreases your risk exposure. Fourth and finally, a professional management team will do all of the trading for you. Their service comes at a cost, but it can cost you less than trading with a broker on your own.

Here is an example of a mutual fund investment. Suppose you have the same one thousand dollars and you find a mutual fund that holds The Cake Place, Macrosoft, Specific Electric, and thirty other stocks. The fund has a sales charge of 1 percent and an annual management fee of 0.5 percent.

When you purchase shares of the fund, the 1 percent charge will be deducted, leaving you with $990 to invest. Your money will be spread across the three stocks you liked and the thirty other stocks in the fund's portfolio. If the manager decides to buy or sell additional stocks, you will only have to pay one fee, an estimate of which is provided before you invest in the fund.

This is no sales pitch for mutual funds! They can lose money just like any other investment, but they allow you to invest in much more than you could have by yourself. The large portfolio can also help you reduce costs and risk.

Real-Life Collaborative Investments

Have you ever done something with another person that you had struggled to do or had failed to do on your own? One example of this that is easy for me to recall is going to the gym. I had set a schedule on my own, but if other things came up, the gym could wait. When I had a workout partner, I was much less prone to cancel or reschedule. It is much more difficult to reschedule for two people than it is for one, and I didn't want to back out on my partner. Exercise is good for me, but alone, I don't like to stick to the plan.

Study groups really helped me in graduate school. When I had to work with other people, I put more time into my studies. Often times, peer evaluations contributed to our grades, but even when they didn't, I exerted more effort when groups were involved. I never wanted to be the weakest link. Splitting up the work made it easier for me to zoom in and have my own specialty. Once the group reconvened, each person was able to explain his or her special contribution to the group. Everyone had to have a broad understanding of the subject, but each person had a unique area within that subject on which they focused.

For example, I participated in a case competition in graduate school. We had a four-member team, and each person had a specialty: supply chain management, marketing, product development, and finance (of course, that was mine). With limited time to study the case and come up with viable recommendations, it was impossible for everyone to become an expert on everything. On a scale of one to ten, I think each of us settled on being a seven on the entire case and a ten on our specialty. This worked very efficiently, because for each question posed to the team, there was always one person with the specialized knowledge to provide a good answer.

It can be hard to accept, but no person can be a ten at everything. My way of dealing with this is to be a ten at something I am passionate about and surround myself with people who are tens in other areas that complement my specialty and augment my knowledge.

In the classroom or in the boardroom, investing with others provides us with a greater base of resources, and holds us accountable to someone other than ourselves.

CHAPTER FIFTEEN: GOOD INVESTMENTS PAY

In the financial world, the term "good investment" is relative. For some folks, good may be nothing less than 40 percent per year. Others may be happy with 8 percent for the same period.

Brokers usually aim to provide their clients with investments that are in the "northwest quadrant." On a graph with risk plotted on the x-axis and returns plotted on the y-axis, the northwest quadrant represents an investment with low-risk and high-returns.

The Risk-Return Trade Off

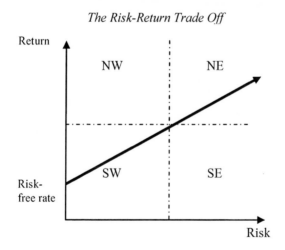

The bold line starting at the risk-free rate of return rises as more risk is assumed. The graph represents the normal relationship between risk and return. An investment that plots in the northwest quadrant defies this relationship.

Risk and return are directly related, so it is difficult to find an investment that can consistently fall in the northwest quadrant. If your broker finds an investment that is capable of this feat, they probably won't tell you about it. It would be most profitable for them to invest their own money and *not* invest yours. If they pass the word on to their clients and other investors catch on, eventually the normal risk-return relationship will be restored. The stock will no longer plot in the northwest quadrant. In layman's terms, the investment will become more expensive, and the higher price will lead to lower returns.

A good investment is one that achieves my personal balance of risk and returns. A good investment is also one that allows me to live my life without constantly checking quotes, and allows me to sleep peacefully at the end of each day.

One of My Good Investments

In November 2008, I visited a neighborhood community center with one of my close friends, Sharon Hayes. We hosted a group of ten teenagers for a program that we call "Real Talk."

This was our second installment of the program. A few months earlier, Sharon, my sister Kia, and I had gone to a local high school to conduct the first installment. One of the young women had enjoyed it so much that she had asked if we would come to her neighborhood and host the program with members of the youth council.

We arrived at the neighborhood community center (a row house that had been converted into a center for kids) with our hands full. We had pizza, sodas, ice, and gift bags for the participants. Each gift bag contained candy, gum, and a packet we called *Food For Thought*. The packet contained a list of tips for effective communication and another list with time-management tips. Also, there was a compilation of quotes on a variety of subjects, including success, hard work, and discipline. Then there were articles on life after high school, how to go about getting a job, joining the armed services, and going to college. The last packet we provided contained common women's health issues, along with their symptoms and remedies.

We spent the next two hours answering questions about boyfriends, teen pregnancy, love, and jealous people. These girls had some serious questions, which we addressed offering our input, but we reminded them that they would have to find their own answers to many of their questions.

Will I ever be able to tell how much good my two hours brought about? I would love to, but investments like these have payoffs that may live on well after I am gone. Out of those ten young ladies, what if one of them changed her mind about going straight to work after school and went to college instead? What if another girl decided not to let a boy pressure her into doing something she didn't really want to do, and so avoided a pregnancy? Do you know how many lives could be affected as a result of these kids changing their minds? I have no clue, and I love it! That is exactly why I am willing to sacrifice a few hours for kids whom I do not know, who may not live in the best part of town. I particularly enjoy reaching out to kids whom other people say can't be reached and are not worth trying to reach—kids who have been written off before they have had a chance to show the world their true composition. Some people say, "Why bother with them?" People are so quick to talk about teenagers, particularly how disrespectful and ignorant they are, but look at the world they are growing up in. Many of these youth only give what they get—apathy and disrespect. Do you know how good those girls felt to have someone talk *with* them instead of talking down to them? Or how good they felt to have someone give them something as small as some pizza with no strings attached? Or the importance of listening to them and helping them find their own answers instead of dismissing their opinions?

> *You'd better bother with the kids today before they end up bothering you later.*

I have digressed, but it really upsets me when children aren't given a chance.

Anyway, this program was held just four days before my thirtieth birthday. For this monumental year, I invited my friends to a small gathering to celebrate. On the invitation, I specifically said, "Do not give me any gifts; your presence will suffice. For those of you who insist upon giving, please donate to my non-profit, The Good Works Coalition."

Wouldn't you know it, some people didn't follow directions! I got money, a lovely robe, two plants, a carved angel, a beautiful tote bag, and a lovely bouquet of orchids. Guess how much money I collected for the Good Works Coalition. Ninety dollars!!!

To the big non-profits, ninety dollars wouldn't grab anyone's attention, but let me tell you why ninety dollars is worth three exclamation points to me.

I gave you the story about the amount of time we put into "Real Talk." Now let me tell you about the money. We fed fourteen people (the girls, the center's staff, myself, and Sharon) and had gift bags for ten young women, all on a budget of $78.

We held the program, expecting nothing in return, but within ten days we made the money back. In the process, we met two graduate students who asked us to return to the center on a regular basis, and who offered to write us into the center's grant for future activities. All of this was gleaned from an investment of five hours (prep time included) and about $80.

So, if you know some kids who are considered not worth bothering with, bother with them anyway. I bother with them because God laid the desire to help them in my heart. My personal reward is making a good investment that God told me to make.

You'd better bother with the kids today before they end up bothering you later. Every thief, addict, or murderer was somebody's child first.

CHAPTER SIXTEEN: THE PAST DOES NOT DICTATE THE FUTURE

Just because something happened before, does not mean that it will happen again. The past may or may not repeat itself, but when a pattern is established, it would be reasonable to expect the trend to continue. Ultimately, it really depends on what trend we are talking about, but in the stock market, it can be dangerous to expect anything.

Stock prices move as a result of information and expectations. If good or bad news is released and it was expected, you may not see much of a price change. When the news was not expected, you will more than likely see a larger reaction by investors.

When you are a company with a good track record, investors come to expect good results, but conditions may change for the worse, and sometimes the company does not control those conditions. The company's executives may publicly discuss their positive expectations, only to later disappoint investors if the company fails to meet those expectations.

This is one reason why, in the investing world, you will come across warnings about forward-looking statements. All publicly traded companies have a disclaimer regarding such statements included in their financial statements. Here's an example of a disclaimer regarding forward-looking statements:

Statements that are not facts, but are based on the company's beliefs or expectations, are forward-looking statements. The statements are based on forecasts and projections at the time the company made the original statement, and you should not place undue reliance on them.

> *Forward-looking statements involve risks and uncertainties, and the company cautions you that a number of factors could cause actual results to differ materially from those contained in any such forward-looking statement.*

Take a look at the key words: "beliefs," "expectations," "risks," and "uncertainties." When I read them, I perceived them to be defensive and negative. This is basically telling people to invest at their own risk, and not to take anything that the company has said or done in the past as a guarantee of things to come.

When it comes to life, I know people who have made a lot of positive forward-looking statements and then failed to live up to them. I also know a lot of people who have set low expectations for themselves and then surpassed them. The truth in either case is that the past does not have to be an indicator of the future. Often times it is, granted, but it does not have to be.

Life is full of beliefs, expectations, risks, and uncertainties, but at any point, each of us can choose to handle them differently. Just because you have been slacking on the job all year doesn't mean you can't try your best today. If you have a habit of being delinquent with bills, you can pay the next one on time. If there is something you have been putting off for a long time, you can start it right now. If you have been careless about how you spend your time, take a few extra minutes now to save yourself a lot of time and energy later.

From Average Student to "Excellent" Teacher

I began teaching finance at my alma mater with an introductory level course called Principles of Finance. I had taken the course five years earlier and earned a "B." I could have done better, but I was going through a tough time that semester.

During the previous semester, my doctor had found a tumor. I took a few days off from my spring classes for doctors' appointments. I went to my doctor and then to a specialist. I didn't care for that specialist's attitude, so I went to another specialist and chose her to perform my surgery. While my classmates and friends were focused on schoolwork, I was preoccupied with blood work and trying to figure out how to make up work. The day after my surgery, I returned to campus and started summer school. My grades turned out well enough, given the circumstances. Then, I spent the rest of the summer working in Washington, DC. By the time the fall semester arrived, I was ready to go back to school. Halfway through the semester, I burned out. I was tired all the time and I was extremely moody. My school work suffered, and I decided to tell my professors what was going on with me. Fortunately, most of them were very nice about it and were willing to work with me. My finance professor was particularly flexible with me and later became a mentor. (After my first semester of teaching the Principles course, I received overwhelmingly positive evaluations, and much of that is due to what I learned from my mentor, the professor.)

After completing the 300-level finance courses, everyone had to take Finance 407—Securities Analysis. We all dreaded that class. I tried very hard, but I just didn't know how to study, and at that time, not many people were holding study groups.

Throughout the semester, I improved on each exam, but never managed to score more than a "B-." The fact that steady improvement led me to a "B-" should be an indication of how low my grades were when I started out. The professor I had was excellent, but he didn't believe in the plus and minus system, so I ended up with a "C" in the course.

In my second semester of teaching, I was asked to teach Securities Analysis. I must admit I was a little apprehensive. I knew I could do it, but I knew it was totally different from the lower level course. What's funny is that I taught much of the 400-level material to my 300-level students. The students I had taught in 311 later went into 407 feeling ahead of many of their counterparts. I found this quite ironic, given the fact that I had the least amount of education and experience in the department.

At the end of my second full-time year, I received the Student Choice Award for Excellence in Undergraduate Teaching. Who would have thought that the "C" student would end up winning a teaching award and a pleasant bonus for her efforts!

I am living proof! Past performance does not have to be an accurate predictor of the future.

CHAPTER SEVENTEEN: FUTURE VALUE DEPENDS ON YOUR INPUTS

Every person places a different value on the factors that affect her life: money, family, job, home, and religion, just to name a few. What is important to you?

Maybe it is money. Suppose you make thirty dollars per each hour of overtime you work, and for one whole week you choose to work four extra hours each night. You will gain six hundred dollars in pre-tax wages on your next check. Now suppose that you arrive home after work on Monday night to find that dinner is packed away in the refrigerator, and your spouse and children are fast asleep. You missed a fresh, home-cooked meal, the company of your family, and an episode of your favorite sitcom. You also missed helping your kids with their homework and getting to tuck them in for bed.

The next night, you get fast food on the way home, because at least it is fresh and hot. Once again, everyone is asleep when you get home. You will have to wait until morning to see your kids.

By Friday night, you are exhausted from the excess work and have a terrible case of heartburn. The next morning, your kids run into your bedroom, ready for you to wake up and get the weekend started with them. You brush them off because you are too tired. No Saturday shopping, going to the movies, or walks in the park for you. You only want to sleep all day.

One week may seem like a short time to you, but look at all you have missed. Sometimes you have to work the overtime hours to make ends meet, but you should be mindful of the things you miss while making extra money.

A week without a parent can be a long time for a child. I

remember when my parents would drop me off for a week at my grandmother's house in Virginia. I cried when they were getting ready to leave me and I cried long after they left. I loved my grandparents, but I missed my mom and dad.

When my parents went on business trips, I worried about them and cried many nights when they were gone. I was talking to my father not long ago and he told me that he remembered the days when he would come home from a business trip and my sister and I would run to him saying, "Daddy, Daddy!" Then he mentioned that now, when he comes home from a trip, the response is much more subdued. We have our own homes, so most of the time when Dad gets back we are not even there. He misses those old days, and so do I.

I love the honesty and freedom of childhood. Kids will not hesitate to tell you how they feel about something and they can get away with it because they are kids. Some kids' quotes I have recently heard and probably uttered myself many years ago include:

"This food is nasty."
"Please, don't make me hug her!"
"I don't like this shirt."
"I missed you, Mommy."
"I want my daddy."

As an adult, I realize that the things I valued as a child are things I still see value in today.

I remember:

Going over to a friend's house and begging my parents to let me stay longer.

Letting my parents know that I loved them by making cards for them that said "I love you" whenever I felt like it.

Being proud of my work because I knew I had done my best.

Making up my own dances, for the sole reason that being creative made me happy.

Writing poems because I wanted people to know what I thought about.

Telling people how I truly felt without trying to save face.

Being excited to go to my grandma's house.

I don't remember:

When I received my first dollar or what I spent it on.

Any amount of money I received that was more (or even just as) fulfilling as any single item on the "I remember" list above.

AFTERWORD

Time is more valuable than money. The value of your life depends on what you do with your time. You have to decide what is most important to you, and it is okay if the list changes sometimes. In an instance when the choice is between time and money, I hope you will give time a chance. Stop spending time and start investing it. By being more careful about the way you invest your time now, you can enjoy the rewards later.

Remember:

1. Recognize that time is a limited resource.

2. Reinvest.

3. Diversify your investments.

4. Keep your word.

5. Be respectful of time.

6. Believe in your investments.

7. Make collaborative investments.

8. Good investments pay.

9. The past does not dictate the future.

10. Future value depends on your inputs.

REFERENCES

1. Based on daily price data from yahoo for December 31, 1979–December 31, 1980. http://finance.yahoo.com/

2. Based on daily price data from yahoo for December 31, 2007–December 31, 2008. http://finance.yahoo.com/q/hp ?s=%5EGSPC&a=11&b=31&c=2007&d=11&e=31&f=2 008&g=d

3. Data from the Federal Reserve Statistical Release records of daily T-bill rates. http://www.federalreserve.gov/ releases/h15

4. Data obtained from the FX Converter. http://www.oanda. com/convert/classic

5. Keogh, B. "Defaults May Beat Great Depression, Junk Bonds Say." http://www.bloomberg.com/apps/ news?pid=newsarchive&sid. 3 December 2008.

6. Siegel, F. *Investing for Cowards: Proven Stock Strategies for Anyone Afraid of the Market.* Beverly Hills: Grammaton Press, LLC, 2001.

ABOUT THE AUTHOR

Tisa L. Silver is a double graduate and former faculty member of the University of Delaware's Alfred E. Lerner College of Business and Economics. She provides market commentary and personal finance tips both through the media and in person. Tisa is also the founder and president of The Good Works Coalition, a nonprofit organization headquartered in Newark, Delaware.

For more information, visit www.tisasilver.com.

LaVergne, TN USA
22 February 2010
173893LV00003B/122/P